Commissioned by Martin Cook and the Chester Music So...
with support from Marketing and Promotional Insi...
the National Heritage Arts Sponsorship Sch...

Spells

Kathleen Raine

BOB CHILCOTT

1. Spell of Creation

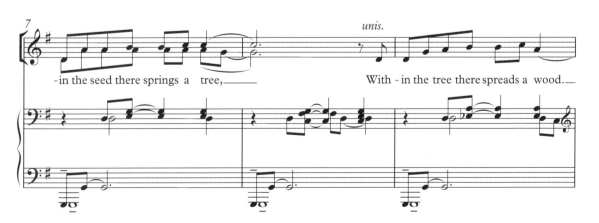

Text from 'The Collected Poems of Kathleen Raine' by permission of Golgonooza Press

Duration: *c.*12 minutes

In the wood there burns a fire, And in the fire there melts a stone,

With - in the stone a ring of i - ron.

sun,_____ A bird of gold._____ With -

_____ With - in the sun a__ bird_____ of gold._____ With -

sun,_____ A bird of gold._____

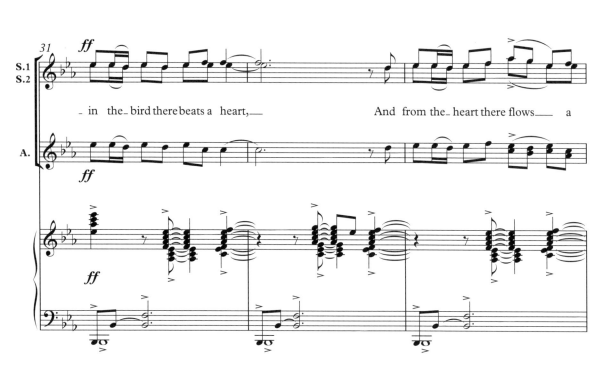

_ in the_ bird there beats a heart,___ And from the_ heart there flows___ a

song,　　　　And in the song there sings a word.

In the word there speaks a world, A word of joy, a world of grief, From

joy and grief there springs my love. Oh love, my

love, my love, there springs a world, And on the

world there shines a sun And in the

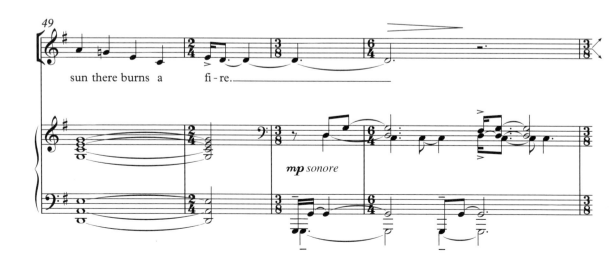

sun there burns a fi - re.

sky and sea with-in an O_____ Lie like the seed with-in_____ the flo-wer._____

2. Spell to bring lost creatures home

ra-ven to its stone,— All birds home!—

Home, home, Strayed ones home,—

Rab - bit to bur-row Fox to— earth, Mouse to the wains - cot,

Rat_ to the barn, Cat-tle to the byre, Dog_ to the hearth,_

Liv-ing to the lamp-light, Old to the fire-side, Girls_from the twi - light, __

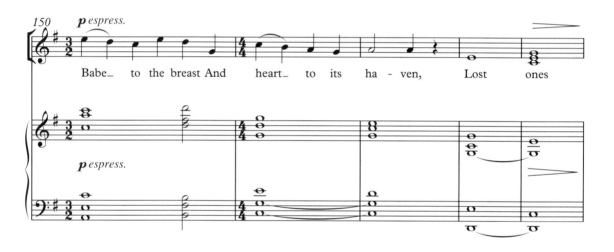

Babe_ to the breast And heart_ to its ha - ven, Lost ones

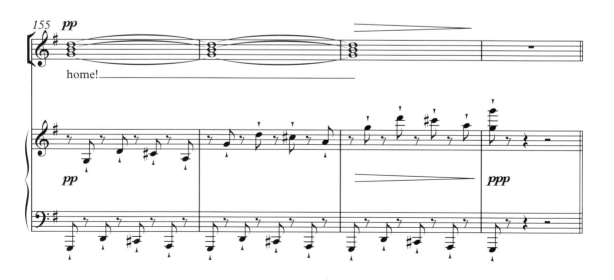

home!_____

3. Spell of Sleep

qui-et wa-ters of night   In— the mir-ror-ing pool of dreams   Where

me-mo-ry re-turns in peace,___   Where the trou-bled spi-rit grows wise

And the heart is com - for - - ted.___

4. Spell of Safekeeping

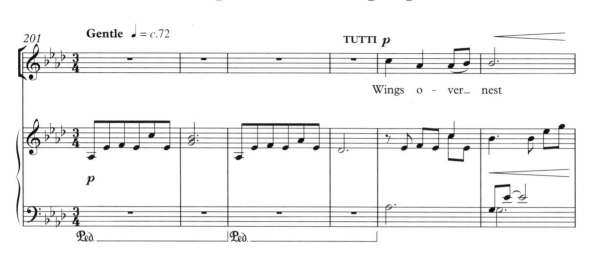

Wings o - ver_ nest

Shel - ter and hide From mouths of night,_____ Rose_ with

green Ca - lyx en - close From storm and rain,_____

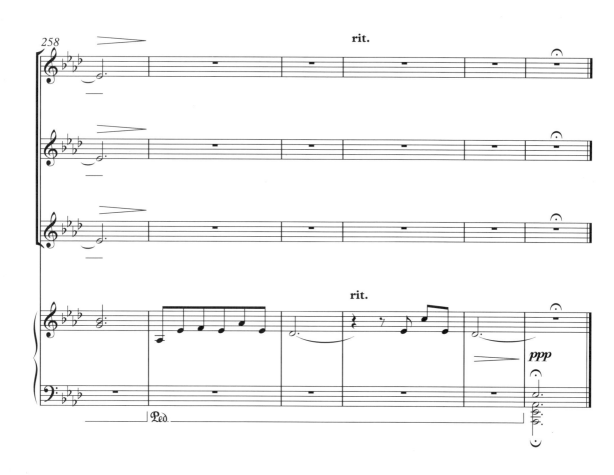